A gift for:

From:

Other books in this series:

365 Happy Days!   The Secrets of Happiness 365
For my Daughter 365   365 Calm Days
For my Sister 365   Wisdom for today! 365

Illustrated by Juliette Clarke
Edited by Dalton Exley

Published in 2014 and 2021 by Helen Exley® in Great Britain © Helen Exley Creative Ltd 2014, 2021.

The moral right of the author has been asserted. Acknowledgements: The publishers are grateful for permission to reproduce copyright material. Whilst every reasonable effort has been made to trace copyright holders, the publishers would be pleased to hear from any not here acknowledged. LEROY BROWNLOW, from "A Father's World", publisher Brownlow Publishing Company, 1965, used by kind permission of John Paul Brownlow. ANITA DIAMANT, excerpt from "Pitching My Tent" by Anita Diamant. Reprinted by permission of the Scribner Publishing Group. Copyright © 2003 by Anita Diamant. All rights reserved. ART KLEIN, from "Dad and Son", publisher Tortoise Books © 1996, used by permission of Art Klein, the author. JENNI MURRAY, from "Memoirs of a Not So Dutiful Daughter" by Jenni Murray. Published by Bantam Press and reprinted by permission of The Random House Group Limited, and by permission of Barbara Levy Literary Associates. MARTIN PLIMMER, from "The King of the Castle" by Martin Plimmer. Published by Ebury Press and reprinted by permission of The Random House Group Limited. ANTHONY QUINN, from "One Man Tango" © 1996, The Anthony Quinn Family Trust/Artists Rights Society (ARS), New York.

Words by: Sarah Abbot, Anjanne Bissessarsingh, Pam Brown, Carley, Phillipe Caron, Jenny de Vries, Pamela Dugdale, Sylvie Dupont, Dalton Exley, Helen Exley, Marion C. Garrety, Charlotte Gray, Peter Gray, Jenny, Stuart & Linda MacFarlane, Siân E. Morgan, Lisa Scully-O'Grady, Paul Raiche are all © Helen Exley Creative Ltd 2014, 2021.
The illustrations by Juliette Clarke and the design, selection and arrangement © Helen Exley Creative Ltd 2014, 2021.

ISBN 978-1-78485-206-1   12   11   10 9 8 7 6 5 4 3 2 1

There is no one
quite like you, Dad.
A one-off.
A Limited Edition.
The dearest,
funniest, kindest
dad of all.

CHARLOTTE GRAY, B.1937

If you love this gift book...

...you can find
other HELEN EXLEY® books like it on
www.helenexley.com

Helen Exley and her team have specialised in finding wonderful quotations for gifts of happiness, wisdom, calm and between families, friends and loved ones... A major part of Helen's work is to bring love and communication within families by finding and publishing the things people everywhere would like to say to the people they love.

Her books obviously strike a chord because they now appear in forty-five languages, and are distributed in more than eighty countries.

Helen Exley® LONDON,
16 Chalk Hill, Watford, Herts WD19 4BG, UK
www.helenexley.com

Dad's love becomes a part of us
that can never be lost.

PAMELA DUGDALE

There are only two lasting bequests we can hope to give our children. One of these is roots, the other wings.

HODDING CARTER
(1907 – 1972)

January 3

I never felt so safe and comfortable as I did in your arms.

ROSANNA DAVISON

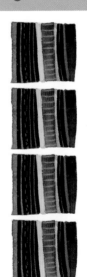

December 30

W hether a man is a king or a peasant
he will always be poor of heart
until he is blessed with children.

STUART & LINDA MACFARLANE

All the best memories
I have, have you at their core.

JENNY DE VRIES

Children are a kind of
confirmation of life.
The only form of immortality
that we can be sure of.

SIR PETER USTINOV (1921 – 2004)

A HAPPY CHILDHOOD
CAN'T BE CURED.
MINE'LL HANG
AROUND MY NECK
LIKE A RAINBOW.

HORTENSE CALISHER

Fatherhood. Two years in and it
continues to be the most exhilarating
experience of my life.
The highest highs and the lowest lows.
From anxiety about your child's
well being that threatens to consume
your very soul, to the smallest
approbation via a smile or a hug
that makes you glow inside
like a thousand suns.

SANJEEV BHASKAR

January 6

"Take my hand"
said Dad.
"See – you can do it."
And I could.

CHARLOTTE GRAY, B.1937

You'd been my guide, father.
My initiator. My elephant. My
deepest yesterdays had been
coloured by you. When I was
very small – do you remember? –
and we walked home at night,
you carried me on your shoulders.
Your shoulders were a ship...
I could reach up and pluck
the swinging stars.

BREYTEN BREYTENBACH, B.1939

The greatest gift a parent
can ever give to a child,
my father gave to us time
and time again – himself.

HANA ALI

It's a frightening undertaking – becoming a parent. To be totally responsible for the development of a tiny human being is an intimidating proposition. It has been said that the greatest challenge to the human mind is a blank piece of paper. Not so. The greatest challenge is the blank slate of a newborn.

KEVIN KISHBAUGH

Dads don't just give their children love – they give them the ability to love.

STUART & LINDA MACFARLANE

Here's my dear dad.
There's no one in
the whole world like him.
And I love every bit of him.

PETER GRAY, B.1928

A father can be a most ordinary man
made a hero by responsibility and love.

PAM BROWN, B.1928

A dad of surprises.
– Maker of sponge cakes
light as air.
Painter of murals on the
bathroom wall.
You have speckled my life
with small astonishments.
Given me laughter.
Taught me how to live.

SYLVIE DUPONT, B.1975

It's different being a father.
All of a sudden it makes you realise even more
what your own parents did for you
and how much you owe them.

ROGER FEDERER, B.1981

A father is the sound of the car,
the tread of footsteps on the path,
the click of the key in the lock –
the arms spread out to catch you.

PAM BROWN, B.1928

January 11

A dad's love wraps us round
and keeps us warm and safe
till the end of our days.

PAM BROWN

 A father is the man
who has finger paintings
pinned up in the office.

CHARLOTTE GRAY

January 12

...there is no greater responsibility
than that of a parent to a child, no greater
bond of love and protection.

JOHN HUMPHRYS

December 21

Dads must have a pretty hard job knowing what to do for the best. We want them to be firm, but flexible. We don't want them to embarrass us, but we love it when they're funny. We want them to be sensitive, but we also need them to be strong. We expect them to understand our point of view, but we're often quick to demolish theirs. How on earth do they cope!

SIÂN E. MORGAN, B.1973

You're a dad in a million – I'm so glad
I was the one to get you.

J. R. COULSON

Of course, my kids drive me nuts and can have me climbing the walls by dinner time, like any parent, but it never makes me feel that I'd rather be working.

MICHAEL HUNT

A dad's love is a child's most precious belonging.
It is unconditional, total, and lasts forever.

STUART & LINDA MACFARLANE

December 19

When you are a dad, you torture yourself over every cough or bout of 'flu that your kids have. Chickenpox becomes a major crisis. I'm a real worrier about my boys. I'm the one who panics when Michael or Daniel get so much as a headache!

LIAM NEESON, B.1952

W e never know the love
of the parent until we become
parents ourselves.

HENRY WARD BEECHER (1813 – 1887)

December 18

Amazing the moment the midwife hands
you over that pink, gooey rat of a baby
(and tells you it's fine that it looks quite so pink
and gooey). It's the greatest moment of your life.
The birth is over.
Everyone is alive. You are a dad.

MATT RUDD

Marrying, founding a family, accepting all the children
that come, supporting them in this insecure world
and perhaps even guiding them a little, is I am convinced,
the utmost a human being can succeed in doing at all.

FRANZ KAFKA (1883 – 1924)

The skies opened
and the rain drenched down.
"Come under my coat,"
you said.
And I watched the storm
from safety.

PAM BROWN, B.1928

January 17

When I think back
to my childhood with you Dad
I can't help smiling.
And I feel again your love
wrap all around me like
a wonderful, powerful,
invisible force.

STUART MACFARLANE, B.1953

How pleasant it is for a father
to sit at his child's table.
It is like an aged man
reclining under the shadow
of an oak he had planted.

SIR WALTER SCOTT (1771 – 1832)

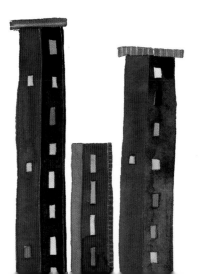

A man can be clever, successful, wealthy, respected yet does not deserve the name of father.
A man can have nothing and be the best of dads.

PAMELA DUGDALE

For you have been there for me,
always; loving me when
I was near impossible to love.
Advising when I could be
persuaded to listen.
Helping me even when I did
not deserve your help.
Believing in me when anyone else
would have walked away.

CHARLOTTE GRAY, B.1937

Through you I learned
how great life can be,
how the simple things in life
are really the most important
and how you treat other people
is really all that matters.

LISA SCULLY-O'GRADY

December 14

There's something like a line of gold running through
a man's words when he talks to his daughter
and gradually, over years, it gets to be long enough
for you to pick up and weave
into a cloth that feels like love itself.

JOHN G. BROWN

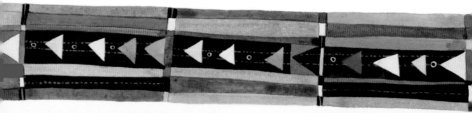

My father was my coach, my inspiration
and my driving force to succeed.

SEBASTIAN COE, B.1956

December 13

To show a child
what has once delighted you,
to find the child's delight
added to your own
so that there is now a double
delight seen in the glow
of trust and affection,
this is happiness.

J. B. PRIESTLEY (1894 – 1984)

How do you thank someone
for love beyond words?
For the sense that I'd trust you
with my life; and that you are
one of the two or three people
that I can truly trust;
that cares, understands ·
and offers (unconditionally)
to help me in my life.

DALTON EXLEY

My father is the standard
by which all subsequent men in my life
have been judged.

KATHRYN MCCARTHY GRAHAM

W HAT DO I OWE MY FATHER?
EVERYTHING.

HENRY VAN DYKE (1852 – 1933)

My father gave me the greatest gift
anyone could give another person;
he believed in me.

JIM VALVANO

My dad was my strength, my true grit, always there for me whenever I needed him.

EDDIE KIDD, B.1959

Whenever I need strength,
I look to you
and somehow a part of it
is passed to me.

SIÂN E. MORGAN, B.1973

My football is really important to me, but my children and my wife are the most important things to me in the world. And that's what fatherhood does to you. You don't realize how much you can love someone until then. It's a totally different kind of love.

DAVID BECKHAM, B.1975

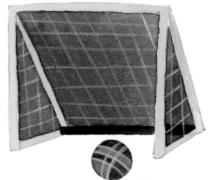

My father believed in
true expression, undiluted by
convention or ordinariness.
When I was little, my father used
to take me on magical walks.
He would point out
the beauty all around us,
a leaf, a stone – everything that
he touched and explained
to me seemed to come alive
and be magical.

ARKIE WHITELEY

Sometimes the best support
a dad could ever give is silent
– times when feeling their concern
will mean more to kids
than words could ever express.

SIÂN E. MORGAN, B.1973

December 8

Nothing is more important to children
– regardless of their age, six or thirty six –
than a father who keeps his word.

CAMPBELL ARMSTRONG

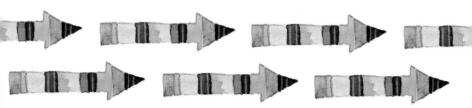

I could stand on my hands. I could walk on my hands. I could stand, bend backwards and touch the floor with my hands and then walk in this position, hands and feet. I could turn handsprings. I could do a flying somersault off dad's shoulders. Off a diving board I could do a one-and-a-half. I could do a half gainer... It was very exciting to be able to do all these things. We had great fun and a real sense of accomplishment as small kids.

Thank you, Dad.

KATHARINE HEPBURN (1907 – 2003)

What my father bestowed
on me was honesty,
being fair with people
and making sure whatever I did,
I tried to be the best at it.

WILLIE MAYS

Kids never forget any times
when dads came home
just in time to help with
homework, to tuck kids
into bed and read a story
or two. Or three.

PHILLIPE CARON

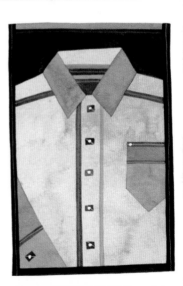

I watched a small man
with thick calluses on both hands
work fifteen and sixteen hours a day.
A man who taught me all I needed
to know about faith and hard work
by the simple eloquence
of his example.

MARIO CUOMO

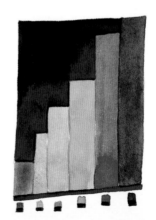

And though I've grown and found my own way – my mind is that of a little child – and I am safe and loved – and home.

PAM BROWN, B.1928

…being a parent
is the most important thing;
more than any piece of work we do,
or any profession.
It puts everything in context.

GORDON BROWN, B.1951

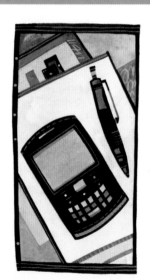

January 29

Dear Dad, Hope the rig's OK and the sea's
not too rough. Mairi's tooth's come out
and Jimmy's teacher says his sums are worse,
and me and Mum think the rabbit's missing you.
But don't worry. Just come home now.

JENNY, AGED 9

Fathers, I was reminded, come in many shapes and sizes and fit no one mold. The good ones have a few things in common, and at the top of the list is just being there. Present and accounted for. There for the big moments, but also there for burgers on a rainy afternoon.

JOHN GROGAN

He was protective, strong, and I could fall asleep knowing that I would wake up safe and sound.

TONY PARSONS, B.1953

Words aren't enough
to describe the delight
[of fatherhood].
My children have
given me the greatest
happiness in my life.

IMRAN KHAN, B.1952

January 31

His hands were indeed big and rough from the manual work he did every day, but for me they have always been comforting and reassuring. Nothing in my childhood gave me greater pleasure than to see his imposing, powerful physique in the doorway, his soft brown hair, eyes sparkling with pleasure as he lifted me high in the air, grinned and planted one of his 'big sloppy kisses' on my cheek.

JENNI MURRAY, B.1950

When a child is born, a father is born.

FREDERICK BUECHNER, B.1926

No matter how old they are, kids feel much safer with dads. They still gravitate towards their dad to help them get back on track if they've lost their way.

SIÂN E. MORGAN, B.1973

December 1

It's a wonderful feeling
when your father becomes
not a god but a man to you
– when he comes down
from the mountain and you see
he's this man with weaknesses.
And you love him
as this whole being,
not as a figurehead.

ROBIN WILLIAMS, B.1952

A father is...
an ordinary man doing his best
to stand in for Superman.

PAM BROWN, B.1928

It was a beautiful summer's day. I'm wearing a crisp, cool summer frock and leaning on Dad as he crouches and I sit on the grass. It's how I always want to remember him – smiling, dependable, with those big warm hands held out in front, always ready to catch me should I ever fall.

JENNI MURRAY

Some gifts can be held in the palm
of your hand – a passport,
a golden trophy or a crystal bowl;
others aren't so tangible,
but are no less valuable.
On the contrary, sometimes they're
worth more than anything else
in the world.
A father's love is one of those
invisible, invaluable things.

MONICA SELES, B.1973

When you have a child,
it's not about you anymore.
It's completely
life-enhancing.

JOHNNY VEGAS

Dad, I love it when
you tell me stories
about when you were little.

CARLEY, AGED 7

November 28

When bairns are young
they gar their parents' head ache;
When they are auld they make their
hearts ache.

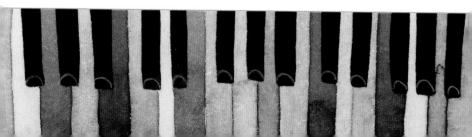

SCOTTISH PROVERB

I could not point to any need
in childhood as strong
as that for a father's protection.

SIGMUND FREUD (1856 – 1939)

W hat I have learned in the process of raising (four) daughters – and perhaps it applies to other human affairs as well – is that there is no single answer, no magic formula, no rigid set of guidelines, no simple blueprint, no book of easy instructions, no sure way of side-stepping difficulties, no easy way out. There is love.

GEORGE LEONARD

If I wanted something from my father,
I would put my little feet together
pigeon-toe style, tilt my head, and smile.
I got what I wanted every time.

SHIRLEY MACLAINE, B.1934

When I was a boy of fourteen,
my father was so ignorant
I could hardly stand
to have the old man around.
But when I got to be twenty-one,
I was astonished at how much
he had learned in seven years.

MARK TWAIN (1835 – 1910)

Dad is usually right. Unfortunately you don't discover this until you've ignored his advice for many years.

STUART & LINDA MACFARLANE

November 25

Every day of my life
has been a gift from him.
His lap has been my refuge
from lightning and thunder.
His arms have sheltered me
from teenage heartbreak.
His wisdom and
understanding have
sustained me as an adult.

NELLIE PIKE RANDALL

The need for a father
is as crucial as the need for a child,
and the search of each
for the other –
through all the days of one's life –
exempts no one. Happy anyone
who finds both.

MAX LERNER (1902 – 1992)

Whether it be for good or evil,
the education of the child
is principally derived from its own
observation of the actions,
words, voice, and looks of those
with whom it lives.

JOHN JEBB

A dad can look quite ordinary – but they are tightly packed with astonishing surprises.

PAMELA DUGDALE

Children are a great comfort
in your old age.
And they help you reach
it sooner too.

LIONEL M. KAUFFMAN

A father is an iconic figure in any child's life,
no matter what he does.

JEREMY HARDY

Don't blame
your parents.
They didn't choose
you either.

ALEXANDER POLA

I'm sure children never really know how many times
their dad has pulled blankets back over them
in the middle of the night.
Or given them his jumpers and coats when it was cold.

SIÂN E. MORGAN, B.1973

I've always loved it that there
could never be
another dad just like you
and that you will always be *my* dad...

SIÂN E. MORGAN, B.1973

He was very special to me.
Whenever I did something
as a little child – learn to swim
or act in a school play, for instance –
he was fabulous. There would be
this certain look in his eyes.
It made me feel great.

DIANE KEATON, B.1946

November 20

Daddy... A terribly busy man but always had time to see me.
Daddy had time for everyone. I have seldom known anyone
who had the depth of feeling for other human beings
that my father had. No problem was ever too small
to bother with, no problem so big that he wouldn't tackle.
He was tall, good-looking, silver-haired, with the kindest brown
eyes. Mother was disciplinarian,
but it was Daddy who could turn
me into an angel with just one look.

MARY MARTIN

A father is the man
who makes a good life
for his children, protects
them, guides them,
standing by them
in times of trouble.

CHARLOTTE GRAY, B.1937

...in bringing up children
and relating to others,
sometimes being is more
important than doing.

CHRISTOPHER REEVE
(1952 – 2004)

$\mathbb{A}$ father is the hands
that hold you safe.

PAM BROWN, B.1928

November 18

A dad's great hands
can calm and comfort,
mend and make.
They are most delicate,
most strong.
Can lift a child to reach
the stars.
Can guide them through
the dark.

PAM BROWN, B.1928

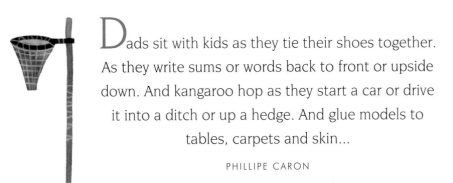

Dads sit with kids as they tie their shoes together. As they write sums or words back to front or upside down. And kangaroo hop as they start a car or drive it into a ditch or up a hedge. And glue models to tables, carpets and skin...

PHILLIPE CARON

I love it that there doesn't seem to be
anything you won't try to fix.
...Even if you're not quite sure how.
That no matter where I am,
I can always call and ask for your help.

SIÂN E. MORGAN, B.1973

February 16

You worship him
as your defender, your hero,
your Big Brave Dad.
Later, you discover
he's really a quieter,
shorter more ordinary man
– and your lifelong friend.

HELEN EXLEY

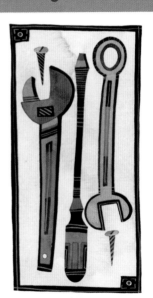

I've wondered, over the years,
as I've recalled these moments
with my father, what they're supposed
to teach me about life. I can't say
there's any lesson, except the sheer
pleasure of his company,
which was a great gift...

SCOTT SIMON

My father holds a cherished place in my life. He encouraged me continually... He gave me the safety, the security, and the consistency to fly as high as my wings would take me.

HENRIETTA DAVIS BLACKMON

November 15

I honestly believe that the most powerful,
penetrating, transcendent form of love
that a parent can give a child is a constant,
repetitive affirmation of that child's essential worth
and potential – even when their current behaviour
would indicate the opposite. Never give up.

STEPHEN R. COVEY

He was a decent
and a gentle man
who showed me fortitude,
love and good humour.

PETER O'TOOLE, B.1932

An essential skill of parenting
is making up answers.
When an experienced father
is driving down the road and his kid asks
him how much a certain building weighs,
he doesn't think for a second.
"Three thousand, four hundred
and fifty-seven tons," he says.

DAVE BARRY, B.1947

A good father
leaves so many joyful,
enduring memories
in his child's mind
like a bank of
emotional strengths
that can be drawn
on through
the testing years ahead.

HELEN EXLEY

I've turned from an ignoramus who knew nothing about children and paid them little attention, into an ignoramus who has an idiotic Cheshire-cat smile from ear to ear whenever he sees them.

NIGEL PLANER

He taught us that we shouldn't
be people of success,
we should be people of values,
because that was the only
thing that endured.

ROBERT F. KENNEDY JR (1925 – 1968)

November 12

I love my little girl an extraordinary amount;
I have, in fact, surprised myself with my talent for fathering.
Since her birth I have been so wholly preoccupied
with the minutiae of her progress – from the growth of
the microscopic hairs on her bald head to the lengthening
of her attention span – that I have been effectively
lost to the larger world.

HARRY STEIN

Father: Someone
we can look up to
no matter how tall
we get.

AUTHOR UNKNOWN

November 11

One of the nicest things about being a father is that you don't have to stop being a son. In fact, there's no way around it. Fathers are sons. The fortunate father/son can draw sustenance from two directions – wisdom, strength, and compassion from his own father, and insight and joy from his sons. The child may be father of the man, but if you look closely into your own son's eyes, you'll probably see your father staring back at you.

JON STEWART

What is sweeter to a man than his children?

MARCUS TULLIUS CICERO (106 B.C. – 43 B.C.)

November 10

A dad's children give him the courage to accept the utter trust they place in him.

PAM BROWN, B.1928

He was a kind,
gentle man,
my refuge whenever anything
went wrong.
He made me feel
that I was very special.

ESTHER PETERSON (1906 – 1997)

A girl's father is the first man in her life
and probably the most influential.

DAVID JEREMIAH

February 24

In the snow dads always
pull you along on the sled,
and they put up a good
snowball fight.
If you're out with your dad
you can guarantee
that you have a good time.
Dads always seem
to make things fun.

K. ABELE

I'm a father and that's what matters most.
Nothing else matters more than that, nothing.

GORDON BROWN, B.1951

As a little girl,
I once sat on my mother's lap
and, speaking my first full sentence,
said of my father,
"Isn't he a bossy boots?"
From family disciplinarian
he has become one of my best friends,
the apple of my eye.

CHARLOTTE BRADSHAW

November 7

Like yesterday Fursey was crying and I picked him up. For some reason, I'm the only one who can calm him down and… man… my chest expands… and all the money, top-hits and fame in the world is nothing compared to the feeling that I can sort him.

FRANCIS ROSSI, B.1949

February 26

When you are a father,
and you hear your children's voices,
you will feel that those little ones
are akin to every drop in your veins;
that they are the very flower
of your life and you will cleave so closely
to them that you seem to feel every
movement that they make.

HONORÉ DE BALZAC (1799 – 1850)

I love it any time when I sink
you pull me up,
and every time you hang in there
until you see the beginnings of a smile.

SIÂN E. MORGAN, B.1973

…apart from all the other things
I have accomplished,
being a good father is really
the most important thing
I have ever done.

JACKIE STEWART, B.1939

A father is
someone who doesn't
only pay for his own mistakes –
he usually ends up paying
for his children's as well.

MIKE KNOWLES

February 28/29

By the time a man realizes
that his father was usually right,
he has a son who thinks
he's usually wrong.

DR. LAURENCE J. PETER (1919 – 1990)

The one thing children
wear out faster
than shoes is parents.

JOHN J. PLOMP

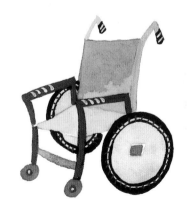

November 4

A proper dad
springs surprises.
Good ones.

PAM BROWN, B.1928

March 1

A good father tries to be wise, kind, just,
loving, concerned, helpful and patient.
He occasionally manages one or two of them
at the same time!

PAMELA DUGDALE

November 3

Fathers are for earning money and helping to keep the human race going.

SARAH ABBOTT, AGE 10

All round the world dads walk,
slow stepping, with their child's
tiny hands clasped safely in their own.
For a little while at peace,
out of the buffeting
of poverty and war.

PAM BROWN, B.1928

November 2

Dads think they're doing a great job until mums tell them they should know better!

SIÂN E. MORGAN, B.1973

What I like best about my Dad is that he is proud of me when I do well in class, and even when I do badly he is still proud of me. I love him for that.

ANJANEE BISSESSARSINGH, AGE 10

My hands remember your hands.
Earth and leaf and scented soap.
A gentle roughness.
Safety.
Reassurance.

PAM BROWN, B.1928

I will never forget all our adventures together.
And I love that you've been the one
to stand in freezing cold gardens, beaches or parks
with balls, rackets, buckets or jam jars
because no one else was mad enough to agree!

PHILLIPE CARON

A FATHER IS THE MAN
WHO WANTS THE BEST FOR YOU.

CHARLOTTE GRAY

Just let your dad be a dad whichever way he can…
that's all you can ask of him.

SIÂN E. MORGAN, B.1973

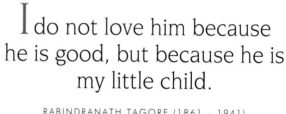

I do not love him because he is good, but because he is my little child.

RABINDRANATH TAGORE (1861 – 1941)

March 6

…my father would pick me up
and hold me high in the air.
He dominated my life as long
as he lived, and was the love
of my life for many years
after he died.

ELEANOR ROOSEVELT (1884 – 1962)

"When you can afford it
you can have it."
Which, dear Dad,
has kept me from bankruptcy
all my life.
It seemed old fashioned
and simply bloody-minded
at the time.
But you were right.
Thank you.

PAMELA DUGDALE

Every dad knows
there is no man good enough
for his daughter.

STUART & LINDA MACFARLANE

October 28

I love all those times I've known
you were there...
But better still, all those times I didn't,
because all that matters
is the happy memory that you were.

SIÂN E. MORGAN, B.1973

I was my father's daughter…
He is dead now and I am a grown
woman and still I am my father's
daughter… I am many things besides,
but I am Daddy's girl too and so
I will remain – all the way
to the old folks' home.

PAULA WEIDEGER

A father is a very ordinary man who must take on the most important job in the world.

PAM BROWN, B.1928

A dad doesn't expect
to be thanked for all the sacrifices
he makes for his children –
so when he hears those special words
the pleasure is all the sweeter.

STUART & LINDA MACFARLANE

A father never feels entirely
worthy of the worship in his child's eyes.
He's never quite the hero
his daughter thinks, never quite
the man his son believes him to be.

AUTHOR UNKNOWN

Sometimes dads can do a good impression of appearing not to care or be upset about something you've said or done, but I can guarantee they do.

SIÂN E. MORGAN, B.1973

There are three ways
to get something done:
do it yourself,
hire someone, or forbid
your kids to do it.

MONTA CRANE

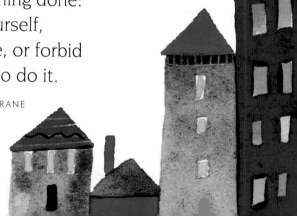

A good dad
understands tadpoles and toads.
And slow worms.
My dad is very good
with newts. My dad likes mice
and elephants.
My dad likes just about
every living thing.
Especially me.

PAMELA DUGDALE

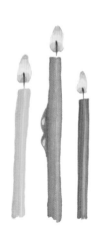

Dad – just one man
yet such a responsibility;
dragon slayer,
financial consultant,
personal chauffeur, magician,
joker, wise man...

STUART & LINDA MACFARLANE

March 12

And you there –
and so… all safe.
My shield from all harm.
Giving me certainty – that safe,
still place to which I can
always turn.

PAM BROWN, B.1928

A wise dad knows
a quiet hug heals most hurts.

PAM BROWN, B.1928

A successful dad is good.
A loving, gentle dad is better.

PETER GRAY, B.1928

October 22

Each one of us needs a protector
a friend, a teacher – a person
who introduces us to our astonishing
planet, with its amazement and
wonders and miracles.
The privileged amongst us are born
with a good, caring father
whois that guide to us.

HELEN EXLEY

March 14

I will never lose the feeling of waking before
the sun and tramping down to the fields with
my father, of wanting to please him,
and to help him provide for our family.
It was a magical thing. It did not matter where
we were or what we were picking.
What mattered was that we had a job to do,
together, and that he needed me.
What mattered was that we were finally
making a life out of no life at all.

ANTHONY QUINN (1915 – 2001)

Dad's maxim on advice:
Don't do anything I did in my youth.

STUART & LINDA MACFARLANE

"Look! Listen"
you said.
And opened up
the world.

CHARLOTTE GRAY

Children need lots of love,
especially when they do not
deserve it.

HAROLD S. HULBERT

With my father life became an adventure.
The minute he walked in the door at night,
even the house seemed to take on a new energy,
like a surge of electricity. Everything became
charged, brighter, more colorful, more exciting...
All fathers are, at first heroes
to their daughters, even when they're
anything but heroic.

VICTORIA SECUNDA

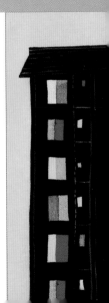

The trouble with being a parent
is that by the time you're experienced
you're unemployable.

H. LESS

I remember my father's final lesson.
My boy will learn by what I am and what
I do far more than by what I tell him.

NORMAN LEWIS SMITH

October 18

...there is one place where perfection
of the heart is given to us in all
its fullness – parenthood.
When you look upon a child
you have been given,
there are no limitations
and reservations. You are looking
with a perfect love.

KENT NERBURN, B.1946

I know I have my father wrapped around my little finger; but he has me wrapped around his.

HOLLY HESTON

Kids never forget any time dads make it,

when they thought they couldn't,

when dads thought they couldn't

...But they did anyway.

PHILLIPE CARON

He has given me
the steadfast assurance
that always, and forever,
I can be sure of him.

BECKY FREEMAN

$\mathbb{A}$ dad with an imagination
and a sense of humour
can survive most things.

PAM BROWN, B.1928

My love for my father has
never been touched or approached by
any other love. I hold him in my heart
of hearts as a man apart
from all other men, as one apart
from all other beings.

MAIME DICKENS (1836 – 1896)

You tried, Dad,
You told me stories.
You taught me how to dance the polka.
You gave and give the best hugs in the world.
And that is enough, Dad.
You are the dad I need – that I love.

SIÂN E. MORGAN, B.1973

It is the family's expectation that will make father into his best and biggest self.

REV. SAMUEL SMITH DRURY (1878 – 1938)

He loves his children not only because everything
in them is lovely and according to his liking,
but because there is a real incomprehensible bond
which is stronger than fiction.

LEROY BROWNLOW

My father was the bright sun around which we revolved. Brilliant, witty, eloquent, he made us laugh and he made us think. And he made us feel cherished in so many ways.

YONA Z. MCDONOUGH

There have been many times
when I thought other people might
be better singers or better musicians
or prettier than me, but then I would
hear Daddy's voice telling me
to never say never, and I would find
a way to squeeze an extra inch
or two out of what God had given me.

BARBARA MANDRELL, B.1948

March 23

"Of course you're scared"
said Dad.
"You'd be a fool not to be.
But get your preparation right.
Take it steady.
Slow, if necessary.
It will come right."
And so it did.
Dear Dad.

PAMELA DUGDALE

October 12

But you know, the most important thing to kids
is simply that dads are there.
And that they try, whichever way they can.

SYLVIE DUPONT, B.1975

A very ordinary man
is a strong
protector in the eyes
of his little child.

CHARLOTTE GRAY

A good dad considers it perfectly manly to say please & thank you.

PAM BROWN, B.1928

A father is the confident, capable, responsible man reduced to tears by a toddler's near-disaster.

PAM BROWN, B.1928

A dad is not remembered by his
children as he is by other people.
They treasure small things,
silly things – the texture of his hands,
the shape of his fingernails –
the balding patch on the top of his head
– the crinkles round his eyes
– his bony feet – all precious.

PAM BROWN, B.1928

October 10

We made our way together to a big tree on the lawn.
He paused there. Then he took my hand he was holding
and pressed it to his cheek and held it there. I thought
at that instant I would never feel unloved again...
There is a sense of eternal comfort,
but you can't express it,
when your heart is in another's hand.

ART KLEIN, B.1923

March 26

A dad who gives his daughter
happy memories to look back upon
is giving her an emotional treasure
to call on at will.
Thanks for the treasure, Dad.

STUART & LINDA MACFARLANE

Dads are there to pull you out of the water
if you start to sink… but they're also there to step back
a little each time so that you have to push yourself
that little bit further.

SIÂN E. MORGAN, B.1973

Warm, funny,
generous, talented,
he was all these things:
but most importantly,
he was Dad.

KATY SECOMBE

Heredity is what a man
believes in until
his son begins to behave
like a delinquent.

PRESBYTERIAN LIFE

You don't have to deserve
your mother's love.
You have to deserve your father's.
He's more particular.

ROBERT FROST (1874 – 1963)

October 7

I can smell him. I can feel his arms. He was a lovely man and he was a nice father, too. Every day with him was a gift. As children we always knew that he was the most important and famous man in the whole world.

GERALDINE CHAPLIN

March 29

…my father had this big belly,
just like a woman nine months pregnant.
I liked him just as he was, fat or robust,
whatever one wants to call it.
People who talked to him about dieting
irritated me – I didn't want less of him.
He was soft to embrace, and there was a lot
of him. I wanted him a lot,
and I wanted all of him.

ISABELLA ROSSELLINI, B.1952

A wise parent never promises till they've checked the bank balance.

PETER GRAY

He rarely raised his voice, but when he did,
my heart would drop through my stomach.

LINDA POWELL

Before I got married
I had six theories about
bringing up children.
Now I have six children
and no theories.

JOHN WILMOT (1647 – 1680)

March 31

I love the animals and the work I do, but when I die,
I want to be able to look at my children and feel
that I have left them well-balanced and wise.
Everything else comes second.

DAMIAN ASPINALL

"Come on" said Dad.
"Keep by me."
Chasing mammoths.
Flying goshawks.
Trudging to work.
Dads have always led us
through the centuries.
"Come on" says Dad.
"Keep up.
You're safe with me."

PAM BROWN, B.1928

Suddenly, a most ordinary
man becomes special.

HELEN THOMSON, B.1943

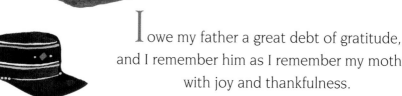

I owe my father a great debt of gratitude,
and I remember him as I remember my mother,
with joy and thankfulness.
I may not have recounted so many
reminiscences of him as of her, but he too
is part of the very fabric of my life.

VINOBA BHAVE (1894 – 1982)

Thank you for holidays.
For games on the beach
and rows about the score.
For cheating at Clock Golf.
For walking us too far.
For losing the way.
For forgetting the keys again.
It was wonderful.

PAM BROWN, B.1928

My dad was always there for me and my brother. I want my kids to have the same kind of dad – a dad they will remember. Being a dad is the most important thing in my life.

KEVIN COSTNER, B.1955

Ⱨow often, when a man,
I have wished when my
father was behind my chair,
that he would pass
his hand over my hair,
as he used to do when
I was a boy.

CHARLES DARWIN (1809 – 1882)

October 1

I love holding him,
the smell of him.
Having him means everything.

ROBSON GREEN, B.1964

When a man becomes a father a bright light illuminates his soul. Suddenly everything becomes clear and for the first time he sees the true meaning of life.

STUART & LINDA MACFARLANE

September 30

A father is a man
changed forever.

PAM BROWN, B.1928

A child
believes his dad
can do anything.
In consequence
he does.

PETER GRAY

September 29

I've always loved knowing that
you'll be there to catch me if I fall.
...That no matter what happens
I could come to you,
and somehow we'd figure out a way
to deal with anything that came our way.

SIÂN E. MORGAN, B.1973

When I was a kid, I used to imagine
animals running under my bed.
I told my dad and he solved
the problem by cutting off the legs
of my bed.

LOU BROCK

It now costs more to amuse a child
than it did to educate his father.

H. V. PROCHNOW (1897 – 1998)

A DAD IS AN ORDINARY
MAN CALLED UPON
TO BE EXTRAORDINARY.

PAM BROWN, B.1928

A loving father knows the difference between protecting and mollycoddling his children. He helps them develop independence – lets them go their own way. But they always know he's there whenever they need help or advice.

STUART & LINDA MACFARLANE

A good dad leaves
trouble at work
on the door step
when he comes home
at night.

CHARLOTTE GRAY, B.1937

September 26

A child on a father's
shoulders finds new horizons.
The scent and softness
of fresh leaves.
The tops of people's heads.
The secrets of walled gardens.
Windows. The thin blue ribbon
of distant sea.

PAMELA DUGDALE

Parenthood remains
the greatest single preserve
of the amateur.

ALVIN TOFFLER

She didn't love her father – she idolized him.
He was the one great love in her life. No other man
ever measured up to him.

MARY S. LOVELL

A man with a family is a lucky man. It is the most valuable thing we have. We give it up at our peril. We break our most solemn and public vows at the price of our self-respect. Our families give us a vital sense of belonging, purpose, meaning, identity.

GARETH WOOD

September 24

Fatherhood is a more important challenge [than acting] and it runs far deeper into what I care about most. If I had to do without acting I'd survive. But I simply couldn't do without my kids.

COLIN FIRTH, B.1960

Dads don't care if you've got
an enormous spot, you wear thick glasses,
forget your lines in the school play,
come last in the races
or don't get promoted at work…
they're there to love you anyway.

SIAN E. MORGAN, B.1975

Teenagers, are you tired
of being harassed by your stupid
parents? Act now.
Move out, get a job,
and pay your own bills
– while you still know everything.

JOHN HINDE

They've always been able to see past
thick black glasses and pimples galore.
Past curly hair, straight hair, no hair,
fluffy hair, pink hair, red hair
or tattoos, piercings and flat feet
To the person underneath
...and love whoever that may be.

SIÂN E. MORGAN, B.1973

September 22

A baby's thumb
is minuscule –
but its father
is firmly under it.

PAM BROWN, B.1928

Children are likely to live up
to what their fathers believe
of them.

LADY BIRD JOHNSON (1912 – 2007)

September 21

If we can genuinely honor our mother and father
we are not only at peace with ourselves
but we can then give birth to our future.

SHIRLEY MACLAINE, B.1934

My daddy doesn't work,
he just goes to the office;
but sometimes he does errands
on the way home.

AUTHOR UNKNOWN

The great person is the one who does
not lose their child's heart.

MENCIUS (371 B.C. – 289 B.C.)

Dads are there
every time kids miss any mark
they were aiming for
...to take them back to
the beginning
...One more time
To start again
And give them hope.

PHILLIPE CARON

September 19

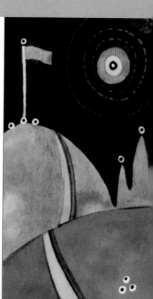

A dad like you doesn't waste time
on bewailing failure.
"Never mind. It was worth a go.
You've learned a lot.
Try something different."

PAM BROWN, B.1928

I suppose that the single most important factor
in my upbringing [was] a sense of security and a sense
of confidence which my father gave to all his children,
and even if I said something foolish,
he gave it as much weight as though it were the most
wonderful insight.

BENAZIR BHUTTO (1953 – 2007)

September 18

The quality of a child's relationship with his or her father seems to be one of the most important influences in deciding how that person will react to the world.

JOHN NICHOLSON, B.1937

April 17

My father wore old, rust-and-chocolate checked shirts
and smelled of sweet briar tobacco and potting compost.
A warm and twinkly-eyed man, the sort who would let his son
snuggle up with him in an armchair and fall asleep in the folds
of his shirt... His clothes were old and soft,
which made me want to snuggle
up to him even more often.

NIGEL SLATER, B.1958

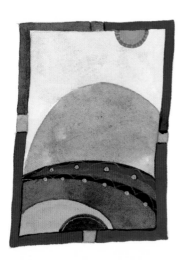

There are no stories
quite like Dad's stories.

H. DALTON, B.1966

After you have children, the balance of your life
changes. The deal is this: their needs, however banal,
come first. You are no longer the most important person
in the world; your needs are no longer (if they ever were),
your wife's priority, they are not your priority,
and depending how winning your child's smile is,
they may not even be your mother's priority.
Children teach you how it feels to come second.

MARTIN PLIMMER

September 16

A very large dad cuddling his
very small baby looks exactly right.

PAMELA DUGDALE

A dad is someone who can get away
with doing things he tells you not to do.

PAUL RAICHE, AGE 14

We all do things we wish we hadn't. Dads are no exception, but for the most part, you can guarantee he was doing it with your best interests at heart, even if he went about it in a way you didn't want him to.

SIÂN E. MORGAN, B.1973

All my childhood
memories are happy
and wondrous.
All my childhood
memories are of great
days spent with you.

LINDA MACFARLANE, B.1953

September 14

When I come home
at night and the two
of them burst through
the door, running down
the walk to greet me,
the world is a beautiful place.
No matter what else
has happened, it's beautiful.

STEVEN V. ROBERTS

One can't possibly know
what life means, what the world
means, what anything means,
until one has a child and loves
it. And then the whole universe
changes and nothing
will ever again seem exactly
as it seemed before.

LAFCADIO HEARN (1850 – 1904)

September 13

You can learn many things
from children. How much patience
you have, for instance.

FRANKLIN P. JONES (1887 - 1929)

A father is the skimmer
of stones, the digger of holes,
the builder of sandcastles,
the flier of kites, the whistler
of tunes, the teller of tales.

HELEN THOMSON

September 12

A father is a man
who has dreams
for his children –
but learns to
adjust to theirs.

PAM BROWN, B.1928

April 23

Something I've learnt
since becoming a parent
is that the pleasure of seeing
my children's victories and failures
are much more beguiling
and moving than anything
I've achieved myself.

ANTHONY MINGHELLA (1954 – 2008)

A man thinks his wife's love
filled his heart until the baby comes
– and he finds there is
plenty of room for two.

CHARLOTTE GRAY, B.1937

Grown-ups never understand
anything for themselves,
and it is tiresome for children
to be always and forever
explaining things to them.

ANTOINE DE SAINT-EXUPERY (1900 – 1944)

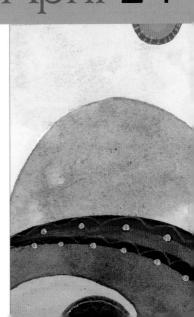

A moment of passion
can make a man a father.
A lifetime of love
can make him a dad.

PAMELA DUGDALE

April 25

A man's children
allow him
to throw off dignity and
be gloriously silly.

PAM BROWN, B.1928

Every girl depends on her dad…
to be her chauffeur, her personal messenger,
her bank manager…

STUART & LINDA MACFARLANE

If you must hold yourself up to your children, hold yourself up as an object lesson and not as an example.

GEORGE BERNARD SHAW (1856 – 1950)

She climbed into my lap
and curled into the crook of my left arm.
I couldn't move that arm,
but I could cradle Ashtin in it.
I could kiss the top of her head.
And I could have no doubt that this was
one of the sweetest moments of my life.

DENNIS BYRD

Children forget that although they have no previous experience of being children, their fathers have no previous experience of being fathers.

SIR PETER USTINOV (1921 – 2004)

September 7

In the short gaps when you are sleeping,
instead of grabbing a few minutes kip like sensible
people would, we tend to creep up and gaze at you,
ostensibly to check that you are comfortable
and surviving, but really just to gloat with pride.

NIGEL PLANER

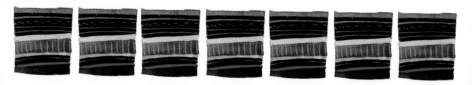

All priorities in a man's
life shift as this little head snuggles
into his shoulder.

CHARLOTTE GRAY, B.1937

September 6

Children never get too old
for a terrible joke or a funny face
— or a rude noise.

PHILLIPE CARON

Even winning the World Cup
is insignificant
compared to meeting your daughter
for the first time.

JASON LEONARD

September 5

A NERVOUS DAD
CAN TURN INTO
A TIGER
IF HIS CUBS
ARE IN DANGER.

PAMELA DUGDALE

April 30

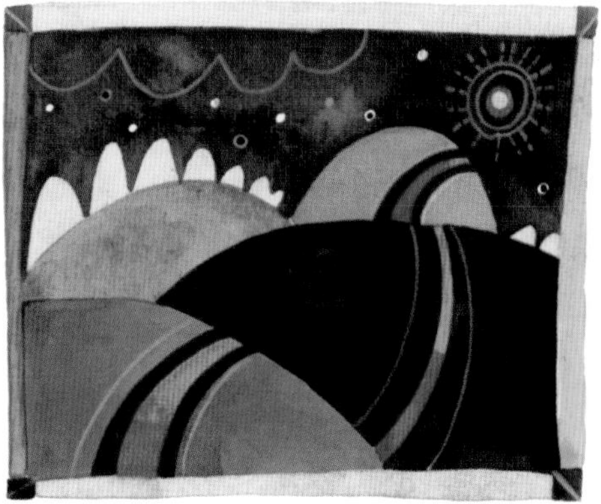

The night you were born,
I ceased being my father's
boy and became
my son's father.
That night I began
a new life.

HENRY GREGOR FELSEN,
(1916 – 1995)

In every real man a child
is hidden who wants to play.

FRIEDRICH NIETZSCHE (1844 – 1900)

A child hires and enslaves you.

PROVERB

Father: A man made strong by love.

PAMELA DUGDALE

When dads have a heart attack
about what kids are wearing,
really what they're saying is,
"I love you and I don't want you to
come to any harm and I'm worried to death
that outfit will invite trouble
and I don't like it that I'm not going to be
there to protect you."

SYLVIE DUPONT, B.1975

September 2

[A successful parent is one] who raises
a child who grows up and is able to pay for her
or his own psychoanalysis.

NORA EPHRON, B.1941

I like my dad,
because when I was five
he would play football.
But now he can't play football,
because he's thirty.

THERON CARNELL, AGE 9

September 1

First and foremost, they are our fathers;
and whatever magic we had with them,
even if for just a few of our very early years,
profoundly affects us for the rest of our lives.

CYRA MCFADDEN

He PROVIDED IN AMPLE MEASURE
WHAT EVERY CHILD SEEKS
MOST PASSIONATELY FROM A PARENT
— COMPLETE BELIEF.

MAX HASTINGS

August 31

He may be president, but he still comes home
and swipes my socks.

JOSEPH P. KENNEDY (1888 – 1969)

Best of all
just when you think things
are really bad...
...Dad pops up
with a funny face and
a terrible joke
and makes you laugh.

SYLVIE DUPONT, B.1975

You had hard times, Dad. I know now.

But never then. You always smiled,

always had a story.

Seemingly untouched by trouble.

How sure and safe my childhood.

Because of you.

SYLVIE DUPONT, B.1975

May 6

Insanity is hereditary;
you can get it
from your children.

SAM LEVENSON (1911 – 1980)

I have found the happiness
of parenthood greater than any other
that I have experienced.

BERTRAND RUSSELL (1872 – 1970)

And there are so many things, lost to kids memories
that they can do because of dads...
...tie shoelaces, fish for tadpoles, annoy Mum, climb trees,
skate, fight against injustice and be polite.

PHILLIPE CARON

August 28

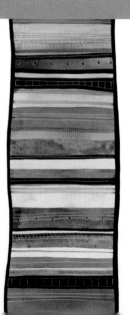

A wise father teaches skills.
Courage.
Concentration on the job in hand.
Self-discipline.
Encourages enthusiasm.
A spirit of enquiry.
Gentleness. Kindliness.
Patience. Courtesy.
And Love.

PAM BROWN, B.1928

May 8

Dads have an amazing way
of seeing their kids potential
and insisting that they can succeed
...with help and practice...

SIAN E. MORGAN

If you want to have power, go into politics. If you want to be a decision-maker, become a consultant. But if you'd rather work like a slave, be constantly insulted and frequently ignored, then "father" is the job for you.

STUART & LINDA MACFARLANE

A dad discovers soon after his baby is born that Things Will Never Be The Same Again.

PAM BROWN, B.1928

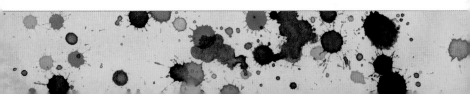

Achild enters your home and for the next twenty
years makes so much noise you can hardly stand it.
The child departs, leaving the house so silent you
think you are going mad.

DR. JOHN ANDREW HOLMES

The first-time father, beside himself with excitement over the birth of his son, was determined to follow all the rules to a T. "So tell me, Nurse," he asked as his new family headed out the hospital door, "what time should we wake the little guy in the morning?"

AUTHOR UNKNOWN

Dad is proud of the buildings
he's put up over the years.
To me, none of these can match
the little things he made just for me
with his two hands.

SUZANNE CHAZIN

Having children teaches us
that we are not the most
important thing in the universe.

STEPHEN GLOVER

The saddest thing that every parent
has discovered since the days of the cave
is that some things cannot be taught.
Every single generation has to rediscover
them all on their own.
And the parents have to stand back
and let it happen.
And it hurts.

PETER DUGDALE

Kids always feel just that
little bit taller
that little bit stronger
and that little bit more daring
...because of their dad.

PHILLIPE CARON

August 23

The people to whom we owe the most never remind us of our debts. They send no bills and they demand no settlement… Why do I write this? Because I am thinking of one of the greatest of my own debts – the one to my father.

EDGAR A. GUEST (1881 – 1959)

The father of a daughter is nothing but a high-class hostage, but when his daughter puts her arm over his shoulder and says, "Daddy, I need to ask you something," he is a pat of butter in a hot frying pan.

GARRISON KEILLOR, B.1942

August 22

My father's memory is a palpable blessing
in my life. It surfaces now and then, an unbidden gift,
like a fish leaping up out of a placid lake.
So it happens that when I marvel at the ability
of the human body to run for ninety minutes
without apparent distress, or listen to a Beethoven
symphony, or laugh at a shaggy dog story,
my father's face appears in my mind's eye
and I am blessed.

ANITA DIAMANT

You see that boy of mine? Though but five, he governs the universe. Yes, for he rules his mother, his mother rules me, I rule Athens, and Athens the world.

THEMISTOCLES (c. 523 B.C. – 458 B.C.)

Few fathers, surely, could possibly
have that brilliant gift
of my father's – he could make magic
in the house by crinkling his nose,
wagging his eyebrows,
or by making Christmas as perfect
as I never expect to find it again.

MIRREN BARFORD

May 15

You gave us your love, your money
and your time. Made things, mended things.
Ferried us for miles.
Thank you for it all, Dad.

CHARLOTTE GRAY, B.1937

A father has his children's absolute trust
– which is a terrifying load for a man to carry.

PETER GRAY

You are my friend
as well as Father,
and that's really special –
to be able to look forward
to walks
and time together
and trips to the Alps
and things.

DALTON EXLEY

August 19

As soon as children arrive in your life,
your house and your eardrums
are no longer your own.
Your pain is distinctly and singularly yours,
but everything else – Time? Privacy?
Biscuits? Kiss them goodbye.

MARTIN PLIMMER

May 17

You take a guy, an average guy,
someone with nothing outstanding going for him.
And there by his side is his kid.
All this kid wants is this guy's eye;
his hand; a look; a hint. The guy touches the kid,
rubs his head, takes his hand,
and the kid looks at him as if he's in heaven.

MARK GREENSIDE

August 18

A father discovers abilities he never
knew he had – to skim stones, bowl googlies,
invent stories, snarl like a tiger, referee,
and soothe a baby into sleep.

PAM BROWN, B.1928

May 18

I have found being your dad the most
paradoxical time of my life to date,
bringing out both the best and worst in me.
Sometimes it made what I thought was
my best seem totally inadequate,
and my worst, quite sensible.
Life, the Universe, all began at last to make
sense at the same time as becoming twice
as confusing and annoying.

NIGEL PLANER, B.1953

August 17

Dads hugs have always
been able to melt away anything that hurts
...And always will.

SIÂN E. MORGAN, B.1973

Parents, however old
they and we may grow to be,
serve among other things
to shield us from a sense of
our doom. As long as they are
around, we can avoid
the fact of our own mortality;
we can still be innocent children.

JANE HOWARD

August 16

Don't be sad that sometimes things
have gone wrong. That's life.
What matters is your love,
for that holds fast whatever happens.

CHARLOTTE GRAY, B.1937

A dad is a man haunted
by death, fears, anxieties.
But who seems to his
children the haven from all harm.
And who makes them certain
that whatever happens –
it will all come right.

PAM BROWN, B.1928

August 15

Dads make children feel as if nothing on earth could possibly hurt them. Thunderstorms and dark nights, weird noises and spiders never seem so scary when dads are around.

SYLVIE DUPONT, B.1975

What children are looking for
is a hug, a lap, a kind word,
a touch, someone to read them
a story, somebody to smile
and share with.

JOHN THOMPSON

To become a father
is not hard.
To be a father
is, however.

WILHELM BUSCH (1832 – 1908)

May 22

You've always been my bridge
to the outside world.
My guide when goalposts moved.
My comedian when I felt blue.
...And my cushion when I fell.

SYLVIE DUPONT, B.1975

I was so tiny when I started playing…
that I would stand between my Daddy's knees,
and I would beg him to get my guitar.
So he would lay it on the bed for me, and
then I would stand up by the bed and play
about three frets down on the guitar.
Oh, I would look at Daddy,
and he had such a smile! I can see it
now, the smile he had on his face
when I would make a good chord.
He would holler, "That's my girl!"

ETTA REID BAKER

Why, if we say we don't really need his approval,
do we keep wishing for it all our lives?

SIÂN E. MORGAN, B.1973

Baby may seem sweet and innocent
but she has an important duty to perform.
She has the difficult job of "father–trainer".
Inevitably, within days of the birth,
Dad will be scurrying around, diapers and soothers
in hand, obeying baby's every
wailing demand for attention.

STUART & LINDA MACFARLANE

Having someone depend on you 24 hours a day
for food, shelter, moral guidance, and financial and
emotional support is not the most rejuvenating experience.
You feel even less young when your baby is not only taking
the car keys, but generating parking tickets too.

MARTIN PLIMMER

A small child knows
every whisker, every mole, every wrinkle
of their dad –
and would not change a thing.

PAMELA DUGDALE

Sometimes when he gets mad at me I can understand why.

MICHELLE WAGNER

August 10

Looking back, retrospectively, the man I now see
my father to have been was of such texture that I would
put him against any man in the outside world.
What I judge him on today would be his character,
his heart, his courage, sense of fairness, compassion,
humanity, on his sense of himself.

SIDNEY POITIER, B.1927

What's the difference between a doctor
and a father? Well, when a doctor
gives you some advice you usually accept it.

MIKE KNOWLES

To his many colleagues and fans
in the world of golf
he may have been a legend
(as indeed I later found out he was).
To us kids, though, he was a father first,
a constant source of amusement,
love, support, entertainment,
inspiration and mirth. Particularly mirth.

RUTH DOBEREINER

Arthur always had his
arms around his daughter
Camera. When he talked
about her, his face would light up
like stars in the sky.
He showed more feeling for
his daughter than I had seen
him show his whole life.

HORACE ASHE

August 8

I might have a sex change operation and become a nun, but outside of that I do not think my life could possibly have changed more than it did by becoming a father. And when my son smiles up at me and breaks into his wonderful toothless smile, my eyes fill up and I know that having him is the best thing I will ever do.

DAN GREENBERG

A father is the man who is more proud
of your achievements than he dare admit.

PETER GRAY

Once Knute demanded
of one of the boys of his age.
He answered, "Seven."
"Impossible," his father said;
"No young man
could possibly get quite
so dirty in seven years."

BONNIE ROCKNE

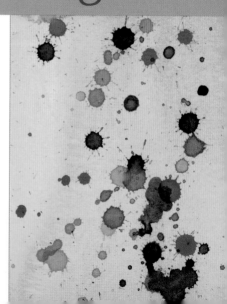

The words that a father speaks
to his children in the privacy of home
are not heard by the world,
but, as in whispering-galleries,
they are clearly
heard at the end and by posterity.

JEAN PAUL RICHTER (1763 – 1825)

August 6

A father is a man
who has a little trouble
recognizing that his children
have grown up.

PAM BROWN, B.1928

Romance so often fails us and so do friendships, but the relationship of parent and child, less noisy than all others, remains indelible and indestructible, the strongest relationship on earth.

THEODOR REIK (1888 – 1969)

August 5

Standing by the crib of one's own baby, with that world-old pang of compassion and protectiveness toward this so little creature, the heart flies back in yearning and gratitude to those who felt just so towards one's self. Then one understands the homely succession of sacrifices by which life is transmitted down the stumbling generations.

CHRISTOPHER MORLEY (1890 – 1957)

Dominating, stern,
protective, my father
had loved me and taken care
of me when
I needed him the most.

ARTHUR ASHE (1943 – 1993)

We should never walk
in the footsteps of our father.
Instead we should walk together,
side by side.

STUART & LINDA MACFARLANE

I have found the best
way to give advice
to your children
is to find out what
they want and then advise
them to do it.

HARRY S. TRUMAN (1884 – 1972)

August 3

When they are born, you find a reservoir of love
suddenly wells up inside you for that little thing.
And, of course, as they get older,
you have reason to be grateful for that reservoir.
I am very proud of them.

RODDY LLEWELLYN

I love that you have already filled my life
with enough laughter to last a lifetime.

SIÂN E. MORGAN, B.1973

To love, nurture, discipline,
and support one's child's growth
requires a perspective that challenges
the full scope of one's humanity.

ALVIN F. POUSSAINT

Children are unpredictable.
You never know what inconsistency
they're going to catch you in next.

FRANKLIN P. JONES (1887 – 1929)

August 1

A father is someone
overwhelmed to find
he is so loved
and so needed.

PAM BROWN, B.1928

Parents are sometimes a bit
of a disappointment
to their children.
They don't fulfil the promise
of their early years.

ANTHONY POWELL (1905 – 2000)

Becoming a father has had an effect on me.
Before, Formula One was the whole focus
of my attention but now it is family first
and then motor racing. I enjoy being a father.
It was tiring work sitting up nights nursing
our daughter when I returned from the first race
in Australia. Tiring – but wonderful.

MICHAEL SCHUMACHER, B.1969

A man prides himself on his strength
– but when his child is born discovers
overnight that strength is not enough,
and that he must learn gentleness.

PAM BROWN, B.1928

When toy guides say "from three years upwards", the "upwards" bit is referring to your dad.

SIÂN E. MORGAN, B.1973

June 6

We do not care how many wrinkles he may have or how his rheumatism makes him limp or how the gray colors his hair, he is still the same great man and the object of our love and adoration.

LEROY BROWNLOW

Get even. Live long enough
to be a problem to your kids.

AUTHOR UNKNOWN

A good dad, a loving, patient, concerned dad, does more to shape the world than most politicians.

PETER GRAY

And when dads don't like your friends...
Really, that's Dad-speak for,
"You're one of the most precious things
in the world to me,
I don't want you to get sidetracked
and I always want
you to have the best of everything."

SYLVIE DUPONT, B.1975

…beyond all the political jazz,
playing the role of father has been
the greatest joy of my life.

PLAYTHELL BENJAMIN

All around the world dads
are doing unspeakable jobs
to give their kids a better chance.
Think of them
with respect and love.

CHARLOTTE GRAY

A father is the man who can heal
most things with a hug.

PAM BROWN, B.1928

You can do anything with children
if you only play with them.

OTTO VON BISMARCK (1815 – 1896)

A baby has a way of making
a man out of his father and a boy
out of his grandfather.

ANGIE PAPADAKIS

I love all those times you've
left the truth for someone else to tell.
Because you thought it was more important
not to hurt my feelings.

SIÂN E. MORGAN, B.1973

It never occurs to a boy that he will someday be as dumb as his father.

DR. LAURENCE J. PETER (1919 – 1990)

July 24

It is amazing how a new child can refocus one's direction seconds after its birth. Everything falls into a feeling of "rightness". I have huge waves of parental love and protection pouring from me…

DAVID BOWIE, B.1947

Am I going to be remembered
as a star or a good dad?
I'll take a good dad any day.

JAY OSMOND

A father is a man
who suddenly discovers
he is braver than he thought
himself to be.

PAM BROWN, B.1928

I love it every time I see that smile
that says you're proud of what I've done.
A small smirk or a big grin
...Or one that grows with time.

SYLVIE DUPONT, B.1975

At the birth of your child,
you forgive your parents everything,
without a second thought,
like a velvet revolution.
This is part of
the cunning of babies.

MARTIN AMIS, B.1949

Nothing escapes when dads
and kids are left on their own
for long enough!

SIÂN E. MORGAN, B.1973

July 21

…look upon [parenthood]
with a sense of mystery and awe.
You are given the joy
of watching life afresh,
and the chance to help
another being take flight
into the richness and mystery
of life. The very clay of which
our world is made is,
for a brief moment, placed
in your hands.

KENT NERBURN, B.1946

It's difficult to explain that feeling.
It's the greatest love affair, an unconditional love.
A protective instinct
was awakened in me.

DANIEL A. POLING

"Just what is it that fathers do?"
"Love you. They kiss and hug you
when you need them."
"What would you like to do
with your dad?"
"I'd want him to talk to me."

NANCY R. GIBBS

Train YOUR CHILD
IN THE WAY
IN WHICH YOU KNOW
YOU SHOULD
HAVE GONE YOURSELF.

CHARLES H. SPURGEON

July 19

Parents repeat their lives in their offspring;
and their esteem for them is so great,
that they feel their sufferings and taste their enjoyments
as much as if they were their own.

RAY PALMER (1808 – 1887)

And dads never seem to worry about their kids
with knobbly knees, unfashionable shirts,
ears the size of plates and scrawly handwriting.
...Because to dads
those things just don't matter as much.

PHILLIPE CARON

I adored him...
and, while I berated him
for his inadequacies in
the domestic chores department,
I found him handsome,
clever, witty, kind, hardworking
and loyal to a fault.

JENNI MURRAY

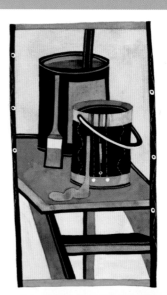

Daddy is standing there, wearing a large
black hat, smiling and calling out my name.
Daddy has come to take me away from here,
to hold me and to hug me and to kiss me
and to listen to me, to play with me,
to pick me up and to whirl me round
and to let me wear his fine,
new broad-brimmed, soft black hat.

PETER O'TOOLE, B.1932

A little child explores its
father's hands and face
as if they were strange territory.
Touching with love each wrinkle,
bristle, bony bit, each snaking vein.
Registering it all as Dad.

PAMELA DUGDALE

June 19

…becoming a dad just feels so right.
I've discovered something very different in life with Taylor…
The best investment you can give in life is to others –
especially to a child. It's a great feeling just investing
your time into this little human being, making sure
their every need is met and that they're loved.

ROBSON GREEN, B.1964

July 16

What greater reward can a man have than to hear his child sweetly whisper "Dad – I love you."?

STUART & LINDA MACFARLANE

A million words, unspoken, tell the love
we have for Dad. A child with a really wonderful
dad grows up with a smile in its heart.

STUART & LINDA MACFARLANE

Dads do glow about their kids' achievements
...no matter how small
...and make sure that other people know
just how proud they are
of what their kids have done.

SIÂN E. MORGAN, B.1973

A father is the man you thought you knew
– but who can go on astonishing you all his life.

PAMELA DUGDALE

A father is a man transformed by love.

CHARLOTTE GRAY, B.1937

June 22

I feel perhaps that you do not think I appreciate
the single-heartedness of your life,
your sturdy unselfishness and the sacrifice
of ambition for the sake of your family.

SIR COMPTON MACKENZIE (1883 – 1972)

A dad will stop to kiss his baby halfway
round the supermarket.

PAM BROWN, B.1928

A dad looking down on his newborn
baby would give it anything,
everything. He little knows
that is exactly what will be expected.

PAM BROWN, B.1928

Whenever I was asked what my ambition was, all I said was, "I just want to be a daddy." I think that is always seen as the primary purpose of a man, to be a good dad. I just can't see how a man can be anything greater than that.

JOHNNY VAUGHAN

Even the roughest, toughest cowboy is transformed
on the birth of his first child. In a midday showdown
the shoot-out takes place between his mean tough self
and his warm gentle self. As the gun smoke fades
the gentle self can be seen riding into the sunset,
"oohing" and "aahing" with baby in his arms.

STUART & LINDA MACFARLANE

Dads are really good at saying
that squiggly drawings
are the greatest.
Even if they can't really tell
what they are!

PHILLIPE CARON

Fathers should not get too discouraged if their sons reject their advice. It will not be wasted; years later the sons will offer it to their own offspring.

AUTHOR UNKNOWN

Your dad is there
to add sparkle and surprise
to your childhood.

SIÂN E. MORGAN, B.1973

A father is a man who places his children above all other achievements.

PETER GRAY

In every dispute between parent and child,
both cannot be right, but they may be,
and usually are, both wrong.
It is this situation which gives family life
its peculiar hysterical charm.

ISAAC ROSENFELD (1918 – 1956)

June 27

No one, me least of all,
could have possibly repaid the care
and thought my father lavished on our upbringing.
A genius of a man, he was the most devoted father,
counsellor and friend, fallible, of course,
but to me entirely wonderful.

TREVOR MCDONALD

A dad never expects
his child to grow up to be his equal –
he always hopes and prays
that she will be much smarter.

STUART & LINDA MACFARLANE

Dads sit with patience and love
as their children try to solve a problem
and quietly guide in the right direction.

SIÂN E. MORGAN, B.1973

Fatherhood for me
has been the most deeply
transformative experience
in my life.
Nothing else
is a close second.
It is a prism through
which I see the world.

BILL GALSTON

The quickest way to get your daughter's attention is to sit down and look comfortable.

AUTHOR UNKNOWN

Dads are a very overlooked and unappreciated species. They stand in the shadows, they get confused as to what to do, and they worry about their ability to be a dad.

SIÂN E. MORGAN, B.1973

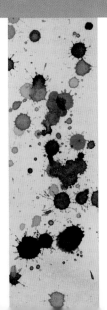

A father is the man
who helps you clear the place up
just before Mum is due back.

PAM BROWN, B.1928

But no matter how old he is,
or how much more a younger parent
could have done, he is my father,
and I would not trade him for the world.

JOHN TAYLOR

A father's love
is shown in hugs and kisses
and songs and laughter.
And food on the table.
And shoes on the feet.

PETER GRAY

Dads are the biggest, bravest, kindest, funniest, most special, best loved friends in the whole wide world.

STUART & LINDA MACFARLANE

July 2

Children aren't happy
with nothing to ignore,
and that's what parents
were created for.

OGDEN NASH (1902 – 1971)

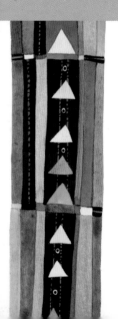

There's no mistaking a parent:
broke, weary, prematurely aged,
but entirely without that febrile preciousness,
that ugly involvement with self,
which to a parent makes another adult
without a child into what's almost
another species, or at least people who live
by a different book.

STEPHEN BAYLEY, B.1951